S0-ATZ-038

Presented to

_____

On the occasion of

_____

From

_____

Date

_____

© MCMXCIX by Barbour Publishing, Inc.

ISBN 1-57748-587-4

All rights reserved. No part of this publication may be reproduced or transmitted in any form or by any means without written permission of the publisher.

Unless otherwise marked, all Scripture quotations are taken from the Authorized King James Version of the Bible.

Scripture quotations marked NIV are taken from the Holy Bible, NEW INTERNATIONAL VERSION, copyright © 1973, 1978, 1984 by International Bible Society. Used by permission of Zondervan Publishing House. All rights reserved.

Published by Barbour Publishing, Inc., P.O. Box 719, Uhrichsville, Ohio 44683
http://www.barbourbooks.com

Member of the
Evangelical Christian
Publishers Association

Printed in China.

Angels

MESSENGERS OF HOPE

Written and compiled by
Ellyn Sanna

BARBOUR
PUBLISHING, INC.

What's impossible to all humanity
may be possible to
the metaphysics and physiology
of angels.

Joseph Glanvill

Angels Unawares

Be not forgetful to entertain strangers:
for thereby some have
entertained angels unawares.

HEBREWS 13:2

> But all God's angels
> come to us disguised. . .

JAMES RUSSELL LOWELL

*I*t may be that angels don't always appear to us in a burst of light and power. The Bible certainly indicates that this is so. We may never know the times that angel wings brushed by us. . .the hand that grabbed us from the crowd just as we were about to slip into the street. . .the stranger whose smile lifted our spirits when we were about to despair. . .the kind word we overheard that told us of God's love and turned our life around. . . These may all have been angels passing unseen through our ordinary world.

In this dim world of clouding cares,
We rarely know till 'wildered eyes
See white wings lessening up the skies,
The angel with us unawares.

GERALD MASSEY

Leo Tolstoy wrote a short story
of a man and woman who
take in a cold, hungry stranger.
They learn much from him—
and then suddenly one day. . .

*H*e was clothed in light so that the eye could not look on him; and his voice grew louder, as though it came not from him but from heaven above. And the angel said: "I have learnt that all men live not by care for themselves, but by love."

And the angel sang praise to God, so that the hut trembled at his voice. The roof opened, and a column of fire rose from the earth to heaven. Simon and his wife and children fell to the ground. Wings appeared on the angel's shoulders and he rose into the heavens. And when Simon came to himself the hut stood as before, and there was no one in it but his own family.

"What Men Live By,"
The Raid and Other Stories

The Angels keep their ancient places
Turn but a stone and start a wing!
'Tis ye, 'tis your estrangéd faces
That miss the many splendored thing.

FRANCIS THOMPSON

*A*nd when the servant of the man of God was risen early, and gone forth, behold, an host compassed the city both with horses and chariots. And his servant said unto him, Alas, my master! how shall we do?

And he answered, Fear not: for they that be with us are more than they that be with them.

And Elisha prayed, and said, LORD, I pray thee, open his eyes, that he may see. And the LORD opened the eyes of the young man; and he saw: and, behold, the mountain was full of horses and chariots of fire round about Elisha.

2 KINGS 6:15-17

Our life may be filled with
angels we never recognize. . .
and we, too, may act as
God's angels in the lives of others
when we allow God's Spirit to use us. . . .

I will not wish thee riches nor the glow of greatness,
　　but that wherever thou go
　　some weary heart shall gladden at thy smile,
　　or shadowed life know sunshine for a while.
And so thy path shall be a track of light,
　　like angels' footsteps passing through the night.

WORDS ON A CHURCH WALL IN UPWALTHAM, ENGLAND

$\mathcal{F}$ ew of us may identify a celestial being during our lifetime (although I am sure each of us has been touched by them). But we can all be angels to one another. We can choose to obey the still small stirring within, the little whisper that says, "Go. Ask. Reach out. Be an answer to someone's plea. You have a part to play. Have faith." We can decide to risk that He is indeed there, watching, caring, cherishing us. . .

JOAN WESTER ANDERSON,
Where Angels Walk

Guardian Angels

For he shall give
his angels charge over thee,
to keep thee in all thy ways.

Psalm 91:11

The guardian angels of
life sometimes fly so high
as to be beyond our sight,
but they are always
looking down upon us.

JEAN PAUL RICHTER

With silence only as their benediction,
    God's angels come
Where, in the shadow of great affliction,
    The soul sits dumb.

JOHN GREENLEAF WHITTIER

$\mathcal{E}$very day from the time my son was a baby until he went to school, he and I would drive by a Greek Orthodox church on our way to one of the publishers for whom I did freelance work. On the front of the church was a huge shining mosaic of the angel Michael. I had barely noticed it, until my son got old enough to talk, and then he would insist that we slow down enough that he could look up at the fierce figure with its glittering sword and tender eyes. "God's fighter," my son called Michael.

My husband and I have always discouraged violence in our home; my children aren't allowed to watch programs where people fight and we've never allowed toy guns in the house. But my son was always fascinated with weapons. "The world's full of scary stuff," he told me once. "How are we supposed to protect ourselves if we can't have weapons?" So he was delighted to find that God had a "fighter," someone who could help protect him from the "scary stuff."

My son's name is Gabriel, and since people are always remarking on his angelic namesake, Gabriel grew up interested in angels. He has a picture of the angel Gabriel hanging above his bed—but as night falls, and fears start to crowd his mind, Michael, God's "fighter," is the angel he loves most.

I don't usually think much about angels myself. But I find I, too, am comforted by the thought that my childrens' angels always have uninterrupted access to their Father in heaven—and if need be, they're ready to fight.

Take heed that ye despise
not one of these little ones;
for I say unto you,
That in heaven their angels
do always behold
the face of my Father
which is in heaven.

MATTHEW 18:10

Before I lay me down to sleep
I give my soul to Christ to keep.
Four corners to my bed,
Four angels overspread:
One at the head, one at the feet,
And two to guard me while I sleep.

TRADITIONAL CHILDREN'S PRAYER

*Guardian angels are
not just for children, though.
Missionaries and other prominent Christians
tell many stories of the times when God's angels
protected them from harm.*

When I was visiting the American troops during the Korean War, I was told of a small group of American marines in the First Division who had been trapped up north. With the thermometer at twenty degrees below zero, they were close to freezing to death. And they had had nothing to eat for six days. Surrender to the Chinese seemed their only hope of survival. But one of the men, a Christian, pointed out certain verses of Scripture, and taught his comrades to sing a song of praise to God. . . .

The next morning, just as the sun was rising, they heard [a] noise. Their fear that a Chinese patrol had discovered them suddenly vanished as they found themselves face to face with a South Korean who could speak English. He said, "I will show you out." He led them through the forest and mountains to safety behind their own lines. When they looked up to thank him, they found he had disappeared.

BILLY GRAHAM,
Angels

The angels. . .
regard our safety,
undertake our defense,
direct our ways, and
exercise a constant solicitude
that no evil befalls us.

JOHN CALVIN

$\mathcal{I}$n 1973, Reverend Stewart G. Michel and his wife, Jenny, traveled to the New Hebrides Islands in the South Pacific to work as missionaries. There they had to deal with tropical diseases, wild animals, and the native tribes. Many of the tribes were open to their teachings, attending the Bible studies that they held throughout the area. One tribe, however, remained unfriendly to them and the gospel message that the Michels brought. They threatened to kill the missionary couple, claiming they had interfered with the ancient tribal customs and that they taught a strange new way of thinking.

After the couple had established their mission and had lived on the islands for about six months, the hostile tribe decided to follow through with their threats. Late one June evening, as the Michels lay in bed, they heard the sound of war cries. The noises grew louder and louder, screams and chants surrounded their home. Holding each other tightly, the couple prayed. "Please Lord, protect us and deliver us from danger." For an hour they prayed for protection while the noise continued. Finally they saw flickering lights.

"Keep praying," Stewart said. "I think they want to try to burn us out."

After another quarter of an hour, the sounds began to

recede, lessening and moving away until they finally disappeared. The Michels relaxed and thanked the Lord that He had delivered them from the angry tribesmen.

Three months passed and the Michels still did not know why they had not been killed that night. Finally, the chief of the tribe that had threatened to kill them came to them, asking questions about their work with the mission and about the Jesus Christ about whom they taught. Some time after that, the chief became a Christian and Stewart Michel asked the question that he and his wife had wondered about for so long.

"Why didn't your tribe kill us that night? Why did you leave?"

"We were going to kill you," the chief said. "We tried, but your guards stopped us and wouldn't let us get to you."

"Guards?" Stewart inquired.

"There were hundreds of them," the chief replied. "They were big men with shining clothes. They carried torches and drawn swords. They surrounded your house and we had no choice but to leave."

The missionary suddenly understood. They had prayed for protection, and God had sent His angels to surround their house and protect them.

Beautiful Angel

Guardian angel,
From heav'n so bright,
Watching beside me,
To lead me aright,
Fold thy wings round me,
O guard me with love,
Softly sing songs to me,
Of heav'n above.

ANONYMOUS

In France, peasants used to say "Good day to you and your companion!" believing that guardian angels should be greeted, too.

*I*n the days of the early church, King Herod had the apostle Peter arrested and thrown into prison for preaching the gospel of Jesus Christ. Not long before this, Herod had had another apostle, James, arrested and put to death for preaching the gospel. Because Peter was arrested during a Jewish feast, his trial was postponed until after it was over.

The night before the trial, Peter was sleeping in the prison, chained between two soldiers. Herod had ordered that he be guarded by four squads of four soldiers each at all times. Sentries stood beside the entrance to the prison and guarded it. Suddenly an angel appeared in the prison cell and prodded Peter in the side to wake him up. "Quick, get up," the angel said, and the chains fell from Peter's wrists so that he was free. Peter walked with the angel past the guards and out of the prison, but he did not know that he was actually free, for he thought he was experiencing a vision.

After Peter and the angel had walked the length of a street, the angel disappeared as suddenly as he had come. Then Peter looked around him and knew that he was not having a vision after all, but that he had truly been rescued from Herod's prison. So he went to the home of one of the church members where many people had gathered to pray. At first the members of the church did not believe the servant girl that Peter was actually at the door, but finally they went to see for themselves and let him in. In joy they praised God for Peter's miraculous release.

$\mathcal{D}$uring World War I the Coldstream Guard was a brave and heroic British unit. One day in 1914 in Belgium, the Coldstream Guard was victorious against German forces who outnumbered them ten to one. That same night, though, the Germans began to move forward again in an attempt to surround the British forces. All other Allied troops retreated from the area with the Coldstreamers covering them; they intended to leave as well as soon as everyone else was out.

As morning approached, the Coldstream Guard was informed that all other Allied units had left and that the Germans were closing in. They were ordered to get out immediately. The unit became disoriented in the semidarkness of a false dawn, however, and completely lost contact with the rest of their units. Realizing they would have to make a stand where they were, the Coldstreamers dug in while they waited for morning.

Although a few members of the unit were hopeful that reinforcements would come to their aid, most of the guardsmen knew that such a thing was impossible. They themselves did not know where they were, so there was no way they could transmit their location. Despite this knowledge, the Coldstreamers were cheerful and their spirits high.

As they continued to dig in order to improve their position, one of the guardsmen glanced up and saw a glowing light a short distance from them. He alerted the other members of the unit and they all watched the light, wondering what it could be. The light grew closer and the men saw the outline of a female figure. They all stared as she came closer. The figure was tall and slim. She wore a white gown and a thin gold band encircled her hair. Wings were folded against her back.

Wordlessly the angel beckoned to the men. At first the Coldstreamers were uneasy about leaving their position, but her motioning became more urgent and finally they all picked up their equipment and crawled out of the fortifications they had dug. Silently, the men followed the angel across the road until they came to a sunken road. They had looked for a road like this earlier, but no one had been able to find even a path in the area. The angel led them along the road to an embankment, where she floated up and pointed at a thicket of trees before smiling at the men and then disappearing. Going in the direction they had been pointed, the Coldstream Guard went toward the thicket, where they discovered two British sentries. They were at the main encampment.

The Coldstream Guard had already been given up as lost, and the other units were excited to see them alive and well. Although their commanding officers searched every map available and the Coldstreamers helped to scour the entire area after it had been cleared of Germans, no one was ever able to find the sunken road that the angel used that night to lead the men to safety.

My Guardian Angel

Dear angel ever at my side,
  how lovely you must be
To leave your home in heaven
  to guard a child like me.

When I am far away from home,
  or maybe hard at play–
I know you will protect me
  from harm along the way.

Your beautiful and shining face
  I see not, though you're near,
The sweetness of your lovely voice,
  I cannot hear.

When I pray you're praying, too,
  your prayer is just for me.
But when I sleep, you never do.
  You're watching over me.

ANONYMOUS

The angel of the LORD
encampeth round about them
that fear him,
and delivereth them.

PSALM 34:7

Behold,
I send an Angel before thee,
to keep thee in the way,
and to bring thee into the place
which I have prepared.

EXODUS 23:20

The Angel That Leads Us into Eternity

Then the angel showed me
the river of the water of life,
as clear as crystal,
flowing from the throne of God.

REVELATION 22:1 NIV

To the angels,
death is only another experience
like so many others
they have shared with you already.

KAREN GOLDMAN

*W*hen people are faithful to God in this world, doing the work He has given them, this makes their deathbed more comfortable because:

They have such peace, even in the midst of their physical death.

They will be in such good company once they have died. The angels of heaven will wait on them, just as they did with Lazarus, carrying them into Abraham's heart. These holy ones conduct everyone on their way to paradise.

. . .those who have been faithful to their God will be able to see the way ahead of them; they know that their future home is filled with peace, and the eternal gates will swing open for them so that they can see into heaven's glory.

JOHN BUNYAN,
The Riches of Bunyan

"I looked over Jordan, and what did I see? . . .
A band of angels coming after me,
coming for to carry me home."

"SWING LOW, SWEET CHARIOT"

*H*undreds of accounts record the heavenly escort of angels at death. When my maternal grandmother died, for instance, the room seemed to fill with a heavenly light. She sat up in bed and almost laughingly said, "I see Jesus. He has His arms outstretched toward me. I see Ben [her husband who had died some years earlier] and I see the angels." She slumped over, absent from the body but present with the Lord.

BILLY GRAHAM,
Angels

Angels offer hope.
Not each of us will receive a physical healing,
miracle, or rescue when we want it,
but a spiritual one.

KAREN GOLDMAN

Are not all angels
ministering spirits sent to
serve those who
will inherit salvation?

HEBREWS 1:14 NIV

The Whisper of Angel Wings

...When the morning stars sang together,
and all the sons of God
shouted for joy?

JOB 38:7

Whisper of Angel Wings

Today I stumbled and once again
Was lifted by an unseen hand.
What comfort and joy that knowledge brings
For I hear the whisper of angel wings.

The guardian angels God sends to all
To bear us up when we stumble and fall,
Trust Him, my friend, and often you'll hear
The whisper of angel wings hovering near.

ANONYMOUS

$\mathcal{A}$s adults we're sometimes much too busy to hear the whisper of angel wings. We live in a world of responsibilities and schedules, weighed down by the details of material existence, and we forget to listen for the quiet voice of wonder, the brief glimpse of glory. Children, though, aren't as busy as we are.

On a three-hour car trip last summer, my family was awed by a display of mammoth purple thunderheads streaked with sudden brilliant flashes of lightning. My husband and I, though, were in a hurry to get home, preoccupied with the responsibilities that waited for us. Meanwhile, my youngest daughter insisted that the sky was full of angels. "They're all around us," she said, her face full of wonder and delight.

I assumed she was pretending that the lightning was the flash of angel wings. But when we arrived home, our trip uneventful and safe, we turned on the television and learned that tornadoes had touched down all around our route. Unknowing, we had found a safe path between more than fifteen tornadoes.

"I told you there were angels," my daughter said.

Around our pillows golden ladders rise,
    And up and down skies
    With wingéd sandals shod,
The angels come and go, the Messengers of God!

RICHARD HENRY STODDARD

Some people say . . .

- that stars are the windows of heaven through which the angels watch us.
- when a raindrop falls on your nose, you've been kissed by an angel.
- thunder is the angels bowling.
- snow comes from the angels' pillow fights.

Millions of spiritual creatures walk the earth
Unseen, both when we wake, and when we sleep.

JOHN MILTON

*The child in this story paints pictures of angels.
She understands that we
do not need to see the sort of visions
that Zechariah and the apostle John saw;
we can still hear the whisper of angel wings
in the ordinary, miraculous beauty that
surrounds us every day.*

*S*he had painted all the angels she had ever heard about. . .the warrior angels with their swords in their hands and flame in their eyes; the seraphs with their six wings, purple and blue wings like the shadows that crept across the marketplace when the first stars shone out and the earth veiled her face in awe of them, covering their eyes before the eyes of God; the guardian angels, less well-dressed than the others, a little overworked and harassed because their human charges gave them such a lot of trouble, but very lovely all the same; and jolly fat little bodiless cherubs like the carvings in her room.

Ferranti, overwhelmed by these portraits, asked Henrietta if the angels really had come in through the window to sit for her. But Henrietta, a truthful child, said she would not like to say for certain; it was true she had heard the rustling of wings, but it might only have been the pigeons, and though she had seen wonderful colors and a lot of billowing whiteness, it might only have been the sunset and the great clouds passing by. . . .

ELIZABETH GOUDGE,
The Sister of the Angels

God's Messengers

And the angel of the LORD appeared unto him,
and said unto him, The LORD is with thee,
thou mighty man of valour.

JUDGES 6:12

An angel is a spiritual being,
created by God without a body,
for the servicedom of
Christendom and the Church.

MARTIN LUTHER

*T*here is a Scripture that I recall just about every time I walk into a Hollywood party or a network meeting: "The Lord is my strength and my salvation. Whom then shall I fear?" I figured if doing the angel show was the right thing to do, then I had nothing to fear. Besides, what is it angels say when they show up with news? "Fear not!"

Angels were messengers of God, not ends in themselves. The angels couldn't be fairies flapping their wings and granting wishes. . . . And at the end of every episode, the angels wouldn't win. God would.

MARTHA WILLIAMSON, writer of the television show
Touched by an Angel

$\mathcal{S}$adhu Sundar Singh was born in 1889 in India. His parents were wealthy and gifted and provided Sundar with all the opportunities they could. They arranged for him to receive the best education available and tried to prepare him for the high social position he could expect to achieve. Throughout his childhood he studied many of the holy writings of the Sikhs, the Hindus, and the Moslems, but he could not discover in them the peace that he longed for. His parents sent him to the school run by the Christian missionaries in the area, as it was the best school around. Sundar hated Christians and the Bible, however, and he made life difficult for both the teachers and the other students in the school.

When he was fourteen his mother died, and by the time he was fifteen, Sundar had become desperate to discover true peace. One night he prayed that if there was a God, He would reveal Himself. If God did not reveal Himself, Sundar had decided to kill himself by stepping in front of the train that passed his house every morning at five o'clock. The next morning he got up at three and took the early morning bath that is traditional to the Hindu and Sikh cultures. Then he went back to his room to pray. While he was praying, Sundar looked up and saw that the room had become filled with a glowing cloud, although everything else was still dark. The cloud grew brighter and brighter and then he saw the shining figure of Jesus Christ in the center of it. Jesus said to him, "Why are you persecuting me? I died on the cross for you and for the whole world." Stricken, Sundar fell on his face and worshiped Christ. After the cloud had disappeared, Sundar went and woke his father, telling him of his experience and that he was now a Christian.

Horrified, Sundar's family tried to persuade him to change his mind and to give up Christianity. When he refused, they poisoned him and eventually banished him, leaving him without home or money at the age of fifteen. He became a wanderer, learning more about Christ wherever he could and telling anyone who would listen about Jesus. As he traveled he became known and respected as a Christian holy man.

At one point in his life, Sundar was feeling rather discouraged as he walked from one village to another. A man traveling in the same direction joined him and walked with him. As they spoke, the man's words so encouraged Sundar that by the time they reached the other village he was feeling much better. At that point he found himself alone. The other man had vanished. Sundar believed that the Lord had sent an angel to encourage him.

Another time, Sundar was walking in a forest in the Himalayas when he came to a wide river that he knew he would be unable to cross. It was getting close to evening and he needed to continue his journey in order to get to where he was going. Night was dangerous in those parts, with all the wild animals around. He looked across the river and saw a fire burning on the other side; a man stood near the fire warming himself. "I'm coming over to help you," the man called. "Don't worry." Then he stepped into the river and walked across to Sundar. He helped Sundar climb onto his shoulders and then carried him back across the river. But when Sundar got off the man's shoulders on the other side of the river, no one was there.

Yet another time, Sundar was in Tibet when he was accused of teaching Christianity. He was arrested and thrown into a dry well which was covered with a locked lid. Many other people had been left here to die in the past, and the well was filled with rotting flesh and bones. Several hours later he heard the lid being removed. A rope came down to him and a voice said, "Take hold of the rope." Sundar tied a loop in the rope and slipped it under his arms. He was hoisted up out of the well where he gratefully breathed in the fresh air. But there was no sign of the person who had rescued him. The next day he stood in the village again and spoke about Jesus Christ.

And I John saw these things, and heard them.
And when I had heard and seen,
I fell down to worship before the feet of
the angel which showed me these things.
Then saith he unto me, See thou do it not:
for I am thy fellowservant,
and of thy brethren the prophets,
and of them which keep the sayings of this book:
worship God.

REVELATION 22:8-9

Caught in our limited material world, we are grateful for the stories that tell us of another world, of celestial messengers that wing across the universe. Angels are amazing, awesome, wonderful. . .but they are created by God just as we are. To worship them would be a little like worshiping our mail carrier, while we forgot to read the letters we received. The message is the important thing, not the messenger. Angels carry God's words to us. They tell us we are precious in God's sight, that we have an important part in creation's story. Most of all, they tell us the Good News: Jesus Christ makes us whole.